EMERGENCIES

Printed in the United States of America.

Library of Congress Cataloging-in-Publication Data
Loewen, Nancy, 1964-
Emergencies/Nancy Loewen.
p.   cm.
Includes bibliographical references.
Summary: Describes the most important things to do when someone is hurt in an acci-
dent and discusses the basic rules of first aid for treating illness and injury.
ISBN 1-56766-259-5 (hc : lib. bound)
1. Accidents--Juvenile literature. 2. First aid in illness and injury--Juvenile literature.
3. Medical emergencies--Juvenile literature.
4. Safety education--Juvenile literature.   [1. Accidents.
2. First aid.   3. Safety.]
I. Title.
HV675.5.L57 1996
613.6'9--dc20   95-25884
CIP
AC

EMERGENCIES

By Nancy Loewen   Illustrated by Penny Dann

THE CHILD'S WORLD

No one wants to get hurt or sick or be in an accident. But sometimes these things happen, no matter how careful we are. That's why knowing how to handle emergencies is important. If you know what to do, you will be less frightened. You might even be able to turn a major emergency into a minor one. Pickles and Roy will show you what to do to practice safety sense in emergencies!

4

Learn how to call for help. In most communities, 911 is the number to call in any emergency.

The person who answers a 911 call (a **dispatcher**) will get whatever type of help you need—a police car, ambulance, fire truck, or rescue squad. But not all communities have the 911 system yet, so be sure to find the emergency numbers in your area. Post the numbers by the phone, and memorize them. Be prepared to tell the dispatcher your name, address, and what happened. Don't hang up until the dispatcher tells you it's okay.

Remember the four W's—who, where, what, and wait.

Practice making emergency calls with your parents. The more you practice, the easier it will be to call if a real emergency happens.

If you are near a pay phone when an emergency happens, remember that you can make emergency calls even if you don't have any money. Dialing 911 or 0 is free and will get you the help you need.

Call for help only when someone is seriously hurt or in danger. You shouldn't call 911 if someone has scraped a knee. But you should call for help if someone is bleeding a lot, is **unconscious**, has a broken bone, or can't breathe. If you're not sure whether or not to call, always call. It's best to be safe.

Knowing how to call for help is the most important thing for you to learn about handling emergencies. But there are other things you can do, too. By learning some basic rules of **first aid**, you may be able to prevent an emergency from getting worse.

For serious cuts, it's important to control the bleeding. Press firmly on the cut with your hand. You can also use a clean cloth—such as a towel, or a piece of clothing—to press over the open area. Keep applying pressure until the bleeding has stopped or until help comes.

If you think a bone has been broken, keep the injured part as still as possible. Moving it could make it worse.

If someone eats or drinks something that could be poisonous, call 911 or the Poison Control Center if you have the number.

With a serious burn, the skin will turn black, white, or gray. Call for help right away, and don't get the burn wet.

If the skin is red, you can run cold water over the burned area or soak it in a pan of cold water. When the burned area feels better, gently pat it dry. Don't open any blisters

If someone near you is choking, call for help.

If the person can speak, cough, or breathe, don't **interfere**. But if the person can't make any sounds, you can try to help. Stand behind the person and place your fists above his or her belly button. As the person hangs over your fists, push inward, hard. This might move the object blocking the air path.

Don't move an injured or **unconscious** person unless there is danger present. Never try to give an unconscious person something to drink.

Sometimes injured people go into **shock**. Their faces might turn very pale and their skin might feel cold and clammy. If this happens, cover the person with a blanket or coat. This will prevent them from losing too much body heat.

Most of the time bee stings aren't emergencies. But if someone gets stung by a bee and swells up a lot or starts to feel **faint** or sick, get help immediately—the person might be having an allergic reaction. While you're waiting for help to arrive, you can run cold water over the sting and apply pressure to the area above the bee sting.

Most snakes aren't poisonous, but a few kinds are. To be on the safe side, if you get bitten by a snake, lie down and stay very still. Keep the bitten part lower than your chest, to slow the spread of poison to your heart.

If someone is having a **seizure** or **convulsions**, make sure there's nothing nearby that could hurt the person. Don't try to keep the person from moving, and don't try to put anything in the mouth.

If your clothes or hair catch on fire, don't run! That will only make the fire worse. Drop immediately to the ground and start rolling around to put out the flames. Cover your face with your hands. Remember: stop, drop, and roll!

No matter what happens, do your best to stay calm. If you feel panicky, take some slow, deep breaths, or try counting to ten. Focus on what you can do to make the situation better, whether that's calling for help, providing basic first aid, or comforting someone who's been hurt.

Remember these tips on handling emergencies and review them with your family and friends. Being prepared for emergencies makes good safety sense!

Glossary

convulsions (kon-VUL-shens)
violent, uncontrolled fit. If someone is having a seizure or convulsions, make sure there's nothing nearby that could hurt the person.

dispatcher (dis-PACH-er)
person who sends messages very fast. 911 dispatchers will get whatever type of help you need.

faint (FANT)
weak and dizzy. If someone gets stung by a bee and swells up a lot or starts to feel faint or sick, get help right away.

first aid (FERST AD)
emergency care. If you know some first aid rules, you could help prevent an emergency from getting worse.

interfere (in-ter-FIR)
to get in the way of, or interrupt. If the person choking can speak, cough or breathe, don't interfere.

seizure (SE-zher)
sudden attack. If someone is having a seizure or convulsions, make sure there's nothing nearby that could hurt the person.

shock (SHAK)
great surprise or great fear. Sometimes injured people go into shock. Their faces might turn very pale.

unconscious (un-KAN-shes)
not knowing or being aware. Call for help if someone is unconscious.